**40 Eye Yoga Exercises
40 Recipes
To Improve Your Vision**

Introduction

- Presentation of the book
- Importance of vision and eye care
- Overview of the book's content

Part 1: Yoga Eye Exercises

Chapter 1 : The Basics of Yoga Eye Exercises
Chapter 2 : Exercises to Strengthen Eye Muscles (7 exercises)

1. Palming
2. Following the finger
3. Imaginary letters
4. Up and down eye movements
5. Circular eye movements
6. Convergence movements
7. Divergence movements

Chapter 3 : Exercises to Improve Eye Flexibility (7 exercises)

1. Oscillations
2. Rotations
3. Zigzag movements
4. Back and forth movements
5. Sweeping movements
6. Diagonal movements
7. Crossing movements

Chapter 4 : Exercises to Relieve Eye Tension (7 exercises)

1. Eye massages
2. Quick blinks
3. Deep breathing
4. Relaxation movements

5. Warm-up movements
6. Inverted palming technique
7. Closed eye technique

Chapter 5: Exercises to Improve Blood Circulation in the Eyes (7 exercises)

1. Blinking
2. Eye rotation
3. Palming
4. Eyelash exercise
5. Looking into the distance
6. Star gazing technique
7. Diagonal movements

Chapter 6: Exercises to Improve Eye-Hand Coordination (6 exercises)

1. Tracking a moving object
2. Ball game
3. Speed reading
4. Reading aloud
5. Eye-hand coordination game
6. Drawing and painting
7.

Chapter 7: Exercises to Improve Visual Concentration (6 exercises)

1. Staring
2. Blurry vision
3. Hidden number technique
4. Hidden letter technique
5. Visual concentration game
6. Eye meditation

Part 2: Recipes for the Eyes

Chapter 8 : Introduction to Eye Nutrition

Chapter 9 : Foods That Improve Eye Health

Chapter 10 : 40 Recipes to Improve Your Vision

Here is the list of the 40 recipes that we will explore in detail :

1. Spinach and nut salad
2. Berry smoothie
3. Spinach and goat cheese omelet
4. Vegetable soup
5. Steamed broccoli
6. Quinoa and vegetable stuffed peppers
7. Grilled salmon with dill sauce
8. Kale salad
9. Zucchini spaghetti with tomato sauce
10. Grilled chicken with vegetables
11. Green vegetable stir-fry
12. Asparagus and spinach frittata
13. Tofu and vegetable sauté
14. Grated carrot salad
15. Vegetable curry
16. Shrimp and vegetable skewers
17. Roasted beet salad
18. Vegetarian chili
19. Cauliflower soup
20. Spinach and goat cheese tart
21. Grilled white fish with tomato salsa
22. Autumn vegetable stew
23. Grilled chicken with mango salsa
24. Tomato and mozzarella salad
25. Lentil soup
26. Spinach and garlic spaghetti
27. Meatballs with vegetables
28. Chicken and vegetable curry
29. Potato and celeriac salad
30. Chicken and vegetable skewers
31. Green vegetable risotto

32. Fresh fruit salad
33. Grilled fish with orange sauce
34. Roasted cauliflower
35. Sweet potato soup
36. Apple and cinnamon tart
37. Chicken chili
38. Cucumber and tomato salad
39. Vegetable fajitas
40. Spinach meatballs

Chapter 11: Fruits to Eat Often for the Eyes
- **Benefits of fruits for eye health**

Fruits to regularly incorporate into your diet for good eye health
- Citrus fruits: oranges, lemons, grapefruits
- Berries: blueberries, raspberries, strawberries
- Red fruits: cherries, currants, blackberries
- Exotic fruits: mangoes, papayas, pineapples
- Fruits rich in vitamin A: mangoes, apricots, melons, cantaloupes

Conclusion
- Summary of key points
- Practical tips for integrating yoga eye exercises and eye nutrition into your life.

Introduction

Book presentation

Welcome to "40 Eye Yoga Exercises and 40 Recipes to Improve Your Vision," a book designed to help you improve your eye health naturally and effectively.

In this book, you will discover eye yoga exercises that can help strengthen eye muscles, improve blood circulation, and reduce eye fatigue. You will also discover healthy and delicious recipes that are rich in essential nutrients for your eye health.

Nowadays, our eyes are constantly stimulated by computer screens, smartphones, and tablets. The long hours spent looking at these screens can cause eye fatigue, dry eyes, and even vision deterioration.

However, with the eye yoga exercises and recipes presented in this book, you can take care of your eyes and prevent these eye health problems.

The 40 eye yoga exercises included in this book are designed to help strengthen eye muscles, improve eye flexibility, increase blood circulation in the eye area, and relax tired eyes.

Each exercise is explained in detail and illustrated with clear images so that you can easily understand and practice them at home.

In addition to eye yoga exercises, this book also contains 40 healthy and delicious recipes that are rich in essential nutrients for your eye health.

These recipes are designed to be easy to prepare and use simple and affordable ingredients. Each recipe comes with detailed nutritional information so that you can understand the benefits it brings to your eyes.

Whether you want to improve your vision, prevent eye fatigue, or simply take care of your eyes, "40 Eye Yoga Exercises and 40 Recipes to Improve Your Vision" is the ideal book for you.

We hope this book will help you improve your eye health and enjoy clear and sharp vision for many years to come.

Importance of vision and eye care

Our eyes are one of our most important organs, allowing us to see and interact with the world around us.

However, despite their vital importance, our eyes are often neglected and subjected to high levels of stress, especially in the digital age.

Indeed, the majority of us spend long hours looking at screens, whether it be computers, smartphones, tablets, or televisions, which can cause eye fatigue, dry eyes, and even vision deterioration.

That is why it is important to take care of our eyes and protect them against damage caused by stress, UV rays, fatigue, dryness, and other environmental factors.

By taking care of our eyes, we can improve our vision, avoid eye problems, and enjoy good eye health throughout our lives.

Eye care includes several practices such as regular visits to the ophthalmologist, wearing protective or sunglasses, a healthy and balanced diet, regular breaks when using screens, and of course, exercises to strengthen eye muscles and improve blood circulation.

In this book, we have gathered 40 eye yoga exercises and 40 healthy recipes to help improve the health of your eyes. We have chosen these exercises and recipes based on their effectiveness and simplicity, so that you can easily integrate them into your daily routine.

We believe that this book will help you take care of your eyes and improve your vision naturally and effectively.

Book content overview

This book is designed to provide you with practical tools to improve your eye health and vision.

It is divided into two distinct parts: the 40 eye yoga exercises and the 40 healthy recipes.

In the first part, you will find 40 eye yoga exercises that have been carefully selected to improve blood circulation in your eyes, strengthen eye muscles, and reduce eye fatigue.

The exercises are easy to follow and require no special equipment, making them accessible to everyone.

In the second part, you will find 40 healthy recipes to improve your eye health. These recipes have been chosen for their ability to provide essential eye nutrients, such as vitamins A, C, and E, zinc, and antioxidants.

The recipes are easy to prepare and include a variety of tasty dishes ranging from smoothies to salads, soups, and main dishes.

Whether you're concerned about eye fatigue, looking to improve your vision, or simply looking to take care of your eyes, this book is an excellent starting point.

We are confident that the eye yoga exercises and healthy recipes presented in this book will help you achieve better eye health and improve your vision naturally and effectively.

Chapter 1: The Basics of Eye Yoga

When we think of yoga, we often think of postures such as the lotus pose or the plank pose.

However, yoga is not just limited to physical postures. Eye yoga, also known as trataka, is an ancient practice that aims to improve visual health and strengthen eye muscles.

In this first chapter, we will explore the basics of eye yoga, including its history, benefits, and fundamental principles.

The history of eye yoga dates back several thousand years. Ancient yogis practiced eye yoga to improve their concentration and vision, as well as to achieve a deeper meditative state.

Today, this practice is becoming increasingly popular due to the benefits it offers for visual health.

One of the most obvious benefits of eye yoga is that it can help improve vision. Regular practice of eye yoga exercises can help strengthen eye muscles, improve blood circulation in the eyes, and reduce eye fatigue.

This can be particularly beneficial for people who spend long hours in front of a computer or phone screen.

In addition to the benefits for visual health, eye yoga can also help reduce stress and improve concentration. Indeed, many eye yoga exercises involve intense focus on a point, which can help calm the mind and improve concentration.

Now that we have looked at some of the benefits of eye yoga, let's move on to its fundamental principles.

The first principle of eye yoga is to practice relaxation. Eye muscles are often tense, especially in people who spend long hours in front of a computer or phone screen.

Relaxation is therefore essential to allow eye muscles to rest and recover.

The second principle of eye yoga is to practice deep, slow breathing. Deep breathing helps oxygenate eye muscles and improve blood circulation in the eyes. This can help reduce eye fatigue and improve vision.

The third principle of eye yoga is to practice focus. Focus involves fixing the gaze on a specific point, usually located at a close or medium distance.

This can help strengthen eye muscles and improve concentration.
The fourth principle of eye yoga is to practice movement.
Eye movements are important for maintaining eye health, just as physical movements are important for maintaining bodily health.

Eye yoga exercises can help strengthen eye muscles and improve eye flexibility.

In conclusion, eye yoga is an ancient practice that can offer many benefits.

Chapter 2: Exercises to Strengthen Eye Muscles (7 exercises).

Now that we have covered the basics of eye yoga, it's time to move on to exercises that can help strengthen the eye muscles.

In this chapter, we will explore seven eye yoga exercises that can improve visual health by strengthening the eye muscles.

- **Palming**

Palming is a simple yet effective exercise that can help relax the eye muscles and reduce eye fatigue.

To do this exercise, sit comfortably and rub your palms together until they are warm.

Then place your palms over your closed eyes and breathe deeply for a few minutes.

This can help reduce eye tension and fatigue.

Finger tracking exercise

Hold your arm out in front of you and track the movement of your finger with your eyes.

Do this back and forth several times, then switch fingers.
This can help strengthen the eye muscles and improve eye flexibility.

Figure-eight exercise

Imagine a large figure eight in front of you.
Follow the movement of the figure eight with your eyes, mentally drawing it several times.

This can help strengthen the eye muscles and improve eye coordination.

Distance exercise

Hold your arm out in front of you and focus on a distant object.
Keep your gaze on the object for a few seconds, then focus on a closer object.

Repeat this several times to strengthen the eye muscles.

Convergence exercise

Hold your index finger a few inches from your nose and focus on it.

Then slowly move your finger away from your nose while keeping your focus on it until it is fully extended.

Repeat this several times to strengthen the eye muscles responsible for convergence.

Closed eyes exercise

Close your eyes and breathe deeply for a few minutes.

This can help relax the eye muscles and reduce tension.

Far gaze exercise

Find a distant object, such as a tree or building, and focus on it.

Keep your gaze on the object for a few seconds, then release it.

Repeat this several times to strengthen the eye muscles responsible for distance vision.

In conclusion, these seven eye yoga exercises can help strengthen the eye muscles and improve visual health. Practice them regularly for the best results.

Chapter 3: Exercises to Improve Eye Flexibility (7 Exercises).

In this chapter, we will explore seven exercises to improve eye flexibility.

These exercises are designed to help loosen the eye muscles, increase eye mobility, and enhance the flexibility of the eye muscles.

Eye Oscillations
This exercise involves looking from side to side while keeping the head still. Eye oscillations are excellent for improving eye flexibility and preventing eye fatigue.

Eye Rotations
Eye rotations involve circling the eyes in a circular motion.

This exercise is useful for improving eye mobility and preventing age-related vision problems.

Zigzag Movements
Zigzag movements involve looking diagonally while making zigzag movements with the eyes.

This exercise can help improve eye flexibility and reduce eye fatigue.

Back-and-Forth Movements
This exercise involves quickly moving the eyes back and forth while keeping the head still.

Back-and-forth movements are excellent for improving eye flexibility and reducing eye fatigue.

Sweeping Movements
Sweeping movements involve sweeping the eyes from left to right while keeping the head still.

Sweeping movements are useful for improving eye mobility and reducing eye fatigue.

Diagonal Movements
Diagonal movements involve looking diagonally while making diagonal movements with the eyes.

This exercise can help improve eye flexibility and reduce eye fatigue.

Crossing Movements
This exercise involves crossing the eyes while keeping the head still.

Crossing movements can help improve eye mobility and prevent age-related vision problems.

By practicing these exercises regularly, you can improve the flexibility of your eyes, reduce eye fatigue, and prevent age-related vision problems.

Remember to practice these exercises with caution and to consult a healthcare professional if you have any concerns or vision problems.

Chapter 4 is dedicated to exercises aimed at relieving eye tension.

Eye tension can be caused by prolonged computer use, television viewing, or even reading.

This can lead to eye fatigue and pain, which can be inconvenient in daily life.

Here are seven exercises that can help relieve eye tension :

Eye Massages
Gently massage your eyes with your fingers in circular motions. This can help reduce eye tension and stimulate blood circulation in the eye area.

Quick Blinks
Blink quickly for a few seconds to help relieve eye fatigue.

Deep Breathing
Take a few deep breaths to help relax the eye muscles.

Relaxation Movements
Sit comfortably and close your eyes. Imagine that you are in a peaceful and relaxed place.

This can help reduce eye tension and help you relax.

Warm-Up Movements
Place your palms on your closed eyes and gently press. This can help warm up the eye muscles and relax them.

Inverse Palming Technique
Sit comfortably, rub your hands to warm them up, and place them on your closed eyes.

Make sure the pressure is gentle and relax for a few minutes.

Closed-Eye Technique
Sit comfortably and close your eyes. Imagine a dark or black color and focus on this color for a few minutes.

This can help reduce eye tension and help you relax.

Chapter 5: Exercises to Improve Blood Circulation in the Eyes (7 Exercises)

In this chapter, we will focus on eye yoga exercises that will help improve blood circulation in the eyes.

Good blood circulation is essential for maintaining healthy eyes and preventing vision problems.

Palm and Eye Rubbing
Rub your palms together to warm them up and then place them over your eyes, with the fingers on your forehead and the palms over your eyes.

Rub your eyes gently with your palms, moving them in circular motions. This can help improve blood circulation in the eyes.

Eye Rotation
For this exercise, sit comfortably and slowly look to the right, then up, then to the left, and finally down. Repeat in the opposite direction.

Palming
For this exercise, rub your hands together until they are warm, then gently place them over your closed eyes.

Sit like this for a few minutes.

Eyelash fluttering
This exercise involves rapidly blinking while keeping your eyelashes firmly closed together.

Repeat this exercise several times.

Looking far
For this exercise, look as far ahead as possible. Repeat several times.

Star gazing
Sit comfortably and focus on an object in front of you.

Without moving your head, look around the object in circles. Repeat in the opposite direction.

Diagonal movements
For this exercise, look up and to the right, then down and to the left, then up and to the left, and finally down and to the right.

Repeat in the opposite direction.

These exercises can help improve blood circulation in the eyes by increasing blood flow and stimulating eye muscles.

By regularly practicing these exercises, you can help prevent vision problems and improve your overall visual acuity.

Remember to take regular breaks when working in front of a computer screen or reading for long periods, as this can contribute to eye strain.

Chapter 6: Exercises to Improve Eye-Hand Coordination
(6 exercises)

In this chapter, we will explore eye yoga exercises that can help improve eye-hand coordination.

Eye-hand coordination is essential for tasks such as reading, writing, drawing, and driving, and can help improve overall vision.

Here are the 6 exercises we will cover

Tracking a moving object

For this exercise, track a moving object, such as a ball or a pen, with your eyes while keeping your head still.

Repeat several times.

Ball game

For this exercise, toss a ball from hand to hand while keeping your eyes on the ball.

Try to maintain rhythm and coordination. Repeat several times.

Speed reading
For this exercise, try to read a passage quickly in a book or online article.

This can help improve reading speed and eye-hand coordination.

Reading aloud

For this exercise, read aloud to help strengthen eye-hand coordination and comprehension of the text.

Eye-hand coordination game
For this exercise, place one hand on your face and try to touch your nose with the other hand.
Alternate between hands and repeat several times.

Drawing and painting

For this exercise, practice drawing and painting to improve eye-hand coordination.

Try drawing simple shapes and filling them with colors.

By regularly practicing these exercises, you can improve your eye-hand coordination and strengthen your eye muscles.

This can help improve overall vision and prevent vision problems related to eye-hand coordination.

Remember to take regular breaks when working on tasks that require strong eye-hand coordination, such as driving or working on a computer, to avoid eye fatigue.

Chapter 7: Exercises to Improve Visual Concentration (6 Exercises)
In this chapter, we will explore eye yoga exercises that can help improve visual concentration.

Visual concentration is essential for performing precision tasks such as reading or writing, and can help improve overall vision.

Here are the 6 exercises we will cover

Fixed gaze
For this exercise, fix your gaze on an object, such as a lit candle or a flower, for a minute or more.
This can help improve visual concentration.

Blurry vision
For this exercise, look at an object and try to make it blurry by relaxing your eyes.

Then, focus on the object to make it clear again.
Repeat several times.

The Hidden Number Technique
For this exercise, draw a large number on a sheet of paper. Hide the number with your hand and focus on finding it by looking at the sheet of paper. Repeat several times.

The Hidden Letter Technique
For this exercise, write a letter on a sheet of paper and hide it with your hand. Focus on finding the letter by looking at the sheet of paper. Repeat several times.

The Visual Concentration Game
For this exercise, draw a grid of dots on a sheet of paper.
Focus on connecting the dots in a specific order without losing your concentration.
Repeat several times.

The Eye Meditation
For this exercise, sit in a comfortable position and close your eyes. Focus on your breath and visualize a white light flowing into your eyes, improving your visual concentration.

By regularly practicing these exercises, you can improve your visual concentration and strengthen the eye muscles.

This can help improve overall vision and prevent vision problems related to visual concentration.

Remember to take regular breaks when working on tasks that require strong visual concentration, such as reading or working on a computer, to avoid eye strain.

Part 2 : Recipes for the Eyes

Chapter 8 : Introduction to Eye Nutrition

Introduction to Eye Nutrition
The eyes are essential organs for our daily life. They allow us to see the world around us and enjoy the wonders of nature.

However, our modern lifestyle can be very demanding on our eyes, especially if we spend long hours in front of screens or in bright environments.

Nutrition plays a crucial role in the health of our eyes. The foods we consume can help prevent macular degeneration, cataracts, and other eye disorders.

In this chapter, we will explore foods that are beneficial for the eyes and how to include them in our daily diet.

Antioxidant - Rich Foods

Antioxidants are substances that protect cells from damage caused by free radicals, which are unstable molecules produced by our bodies in response to stress and pollution.

Free radicals can cause damage to the cells of our eyes, which can lead to vision problems.
Antioxidant - rich foods include colorful fruits and vegetables, such as carrots, spinach, red and yellow peppers, oranges, berries, and grapes.

Nuts and seeds, particularly almonds, Brazil nuts, and sunflower seeds, are also high in antioxidants.

Omega - 3 Fatty Acids

Omega-3 fatty acids are healthy fats that our body cannot produce on its own, which means we need to obtain them from our diet.

Omega-3 fatty acids have been linked to a reduced risk of age-related macular degeneration and dry eye.

Foods rich in omega-3 fatty acids include fatty fish, such as salmon, mackerel, and sardines, as well as nuts and seeds, such as flaxseeds and walnuts.

Vitamin A

Vitamin A is an important vitamin for eye health. It is necessary for the production of retinal pigments, which are essential for night vision.

Vitamin A deficiency can cause night blindness.

Foods rich in vitamin A include carrots, sweet potatoes, spinach, and fruits such as mangoes and melons.

Vitamin C
Vitamin C is a powerful antioxidant that protects cells from damage by free radicals.

It is also important for the health of the blood vessels in the eye.
Foods rich in vitamin C include citrus fruits, kiwis, berries, red peppers, and spinach.

Vitamin E
Foods rich in vitamin E include nuts, seeds, avocados, spinach, and vegetable oils.

Flavonoids
Flavonoids are plant compounds that have antioxidant properties.

They can help protect eye cells against damage from free radicals and reduce the risk of eye diseases.

Foods rich in flavonoids include green tea, cocoa, citrus fruits, and berries.

Foods to avoid
Some foods can be harmful to the eyes. Foods high in saturated fat, such as red meat and dairy products, can increase the risk of age-related macular degeneration.

Foods high in sugar can also be harmful to the eyes, increasing the risk of cataracts and macular degeneration.

Conclusion
Nutrition plays a crucial role in eye health.

Foods rich in antioxidants, omega-3 fatty acids, vitamins A, C, and E, as well as flavonoids, can help protect eye cells against damage from free radicals and reduce the risk of eye diseases.

By avoiding foods high in saturated fat and sugar, we can also help preserve the health of our eyes.

By including these foods in our daily diet, we can improve the health of our eyes and enjoy clear and sharp vision throughout our lives.

Chapter 9: Foods that Improve Eye Health

The foods we consume have a significant impact on our eye health.
A healthy and balanced diet can help improve eye health and reduce the risk of eye diseases such as age-related macular degeneration, cataracts, and dry eyes.

In this chapter, we will examine some of the best foods for eye health.

Leafy Green Vegetables

Leafy green vegetables such as spinach, kale, and arugula are rich in antioxidants such as lutein and zeaxanthin.

These antioxidants help protect the cells in the eyes against damage from free radicals and reduce the risk of age-related macular degeneration.

Leafy green vegetables are also rich in vitamins A, C, and E, which are important for eye health.

Carrots

Carrots are rich in beta-carotene, an antioxidant that converts to vitamin A in the body.

Vitamin A is important for eye health because it helps protect the surface of the eyes and maintain clear vision.
Carrots are also rich in lutein and zeaxanthin, which are important for eye health.

Citrus Fruits

Citrus fruits such as oranges, tangerines, and grapefruits are rich in vitamin C, an antioxidant that helps protect the cells in the eyes against damage from free radicals.

Vitamin C is also important for the health of the blood vessels in the eyes.

Berries
Berries such as blueberries, strawberries, and raspberries are rich in anthocyanins, an antioxidant that helps protect the cells in the eyes against damage from free radicals and reduces the risk of age-related macular degeneration.

Nuts and Seeds
Nuts and seeds are rich in omega-3 fatty acids, which are important for eye health.

Omega-3 fatty acids help reduce inflammation in the eyes and may reduce the risk of age-related macular degeneration and dry eye.

Nuts and seeds are also rich in vitamin E, an important antioxidant for eye health.

Fish
Fish is an excellent source of omega-3 fatty acids, particularly salmon, tuna, and sardines.

Omega-3 fatty acids help reduce inflammation in the eyes and may reduce the risk of age-related macular degeneration and dry eye.

Green Tea

Green tea is rich in flavonoids, an antioxidant that helps protect the cells in the eyes against damage from free radicals.

Flavonoids in green tea have also been associated with a reduced risk of cataracts and age-related macular degeneration.

Eggs

Eggs are rich in lutein and zeaxanthin, which are important for eye health. Lutein and zeaxanthin are found in the colored part of the eye called the macula and help protect macular cells against damage from free radicals.

Foods Rich in Zinc
Zinc is an important mineral for eye health. It helps transport vitamin A from the body's storage organs to the retina, where it is used to produce the visual pigment rhodopsin.

Foods rich in zinc include oysters, beef, pork, chicken, beans, and nuts. In conclusion, a healthy and balanced diet is important for eye health.

Leafy green vegetables, carrots, citrus fruits, berries, nuts and seeds, fish, green tea, eggs, and zinc-rich foods are all foods that can help improve eye health.

Incorporating these foods into your diet can help protect your eyes against free radical damage and reduce the risk of eye diseases.

Chapter 10 : 40 Recipes to Improve Your Vision
In this chapter, I will introduce you to 40 recipes to improve your vision.

These recipes are intended to be used in addition to the eye yoga exercises you learned in the previous chapters.

The recipes are all based on nutrient-rich and antioxidant-rich foods, which are essential for maintaining healthy vision.

Here is the list of 40 recipes that we will explore in detail :

1. Spinach and nut salad
2. Berry smoothie
3. Spinach and goat cheese omelet
4. Vegetable soup
5. Steamed broccoli

6. Quinoa and vegetable stuffed peppers
7. Grilled salmon with dill sauce
8. Kale salad
9. Zucchini spaghetti with tomato sauce
10. Grilled chicken with vegetables
11. Green vegetable stir-fry
12. Asparagus and spinach frittata
13. Tofu and vegetable stir-fry
14. Shredded carrot salad
15. Vegetable curry
16. Shrimp and vegetable skewers
17. Roasted beet salad
18. Vegetarian chili
19. Cauliflower soup
20. Spinach and Goat Cheese Tart
21. Grilled White Fish with Tomato Salsa
22. Fall Vegetable Stew
23. Grilled Chicken with Mango Salsa
24. Tomato and Mozzarella Salad
25. Coral Lentil Soup
26. Spaghetti with Spinach and Garlic
27. Meatballs with Vegetables
28. Chicken Curry with Vegetables
29. Potato and Celery Root Salad
30. Chicken and Vegetable Skewers
31. Green Vegetable Risotto
32. Fresh Fruit Salad
33. Grilled Fish with Orange Sauce
34. Roasted Cauliflower
35. Sweet Potato Soup
36. Apple and Cinnamon Tart
37. Chicken Chili
38. Cucumber and Tomato Salad
39. Vegetable Fajitas
40. Spinach Meatballs

Each recipe will be presented with a list of ingredients and step-by-step instructions for preparation.

Additionally, I will provide information on the nutrients and antioxidants present in each dish and how they can help improve your vision.

Ready to discover these delicious recipes for improving your vision?

Join me in the upcoming chapters to learn all about the benefits of each recipe and how to prepare them at home.

Spinach and Walnut Salad
- Ingredients :

4 cups fresh spinach
1/4 cup chopped walnuts
1/4 cup raisins
1/4 cup crumbled goat cheese
1/4 cup balsamic vinaigrette

- Instructions :

Wash and drain fresh spinach.
Chop walnuts and set aside.

In a large bowl, mix fresh spinach with raisins.
Add crumbled goat cheese and mix gently.
Add chopped walnuts and mix again.

Drizzle the salad with balsamic vinaigrette and mix to coat all

- Nutrients and Antioxidants Present in Spinach and Walnut Salad :

Fresh spinach is rich in lutein and zeaxanthin, two antioxidants that help protect eyes from damage caused by free radicals.

Walnuts are an excellent source of omega-3 fatty acids, which can help reduce inflammation in the eyes and improve blood circulation.

Raisins are rich in polyphenols, a type of antioxidant that can help reduce inflammation in the eyes and protect cells from damage.

Goat cheese is a good source of vitamin A, which is essential for maintaining healthy vision.

Balsamic vinaigrette contains antioxidants such as polyphenols, which can help protect eyes from damage caused by free radicals.

In conclusion, spinach and walnut salad is a delicious way to get important nutrients and antioxidants to maintain healthy vision.

It is easy to prepare and can be served as an appetizer or main course. Try it today and see for yourself how it can improve your vision and overall health.

Berry Smoothie

Ingredients:

- 1/2 cup fresh or frozen blueberries
- 1/2 cup fresh or frozen strawberries
- 1 ripe banana
- 1/2 cup unsweetened almond milk
- 1/2 cup nonfat Greek yogurt
- 1 tablespoon honey
- 1 tablespoon chia seeds

Instructions:

1. In a blender, blend blueberries, strawberries, and banana until smooth.
2. Add almond milk and Greek yogurt, and blend again until well combined.
3. Add honey and chia seeds, and blend once more to mix all ingredients.
4. Serve the fresh smoothie in a tall glass or bowl.

Nutrients and antioxidants in the berry smoothie:

- Blueberries and strawberries are rich in vitamin C, an antioxidant that helps prevent free radical damage in the eyes.

- Bananas are rich in potassium, an important nutrient that may help regulate blood pressure in the eyes and improve blood circulation.
- Almond milk is rich in vitamin E, an antioxidant that may help protect the eyes against free radical damage and prevent age-related macular degeneration.
- Greek yogurt is rich in protein, which helps maintain eye tissue health and improve vision.
- Honey is rich in flavonoids, antioxidants that may help reduce inflammation in the eyes and improve overall eye health.
- Chia seeds are rich in omega-3 fatty acids, which may help improve blood circulation in the eyes and prevent age-related eye diseases.

1. In conclusion, this berry smoothie is a healthy and delicious drink that is also beneficial for eye health. The ingredients are rich in nutrients and antioxidants that can help protect the eyes against free radical damage, improve blood circulation, and maintain overall eye tissue health. Try this simple and tasty recipe for a refreshing and nutritious snack that can help improve your vision.

2. Spinach and Goat Cheese Omelette

Ingredients:

- 2 eggs
- 1/4 cup chopped fresh spinach
- 1/4 cup crumbled goat cheese
- 1/4 cup unsweetened almond milk
- 1 tablespoon olive oil
- Salt and pepper, to taste

Instructions:

1. In a bowl, beat the eggs with almond milk until smooth. Add salt and pepper to taste.
2. In a pan, heat olive oil over medium heat. Add chopped spinach and sauté for about 1 minute until tender.

3. Pour the egg mixture into the pan and let it cook for 1-2 minutes. Add the crumbled goat cheese on one half of the omelette.
4. Using a spatula, fold the omelette in half to cover the goat cheese. Let it cook for another 1-2 minutes until the omelette is golden and the cheese is melted.
5. Serve hot.

Nutrients and antioxidants in spinach and goat cheese omelette:

- Eggs are rich in lutein and zeaxanthin, two antioxidants that help prevent damage caused by free radicals in the eyes and reduce the risk of age-related macular degeneration.
- Spinach is rich in vitamin C and beta-carotene, antioxidants that can help protect the eyes against damage caused by free radicals and prevent macular degeneration.
- Goat cheese is rich in vitamin A, an important nutrient for eye health that can help prevent dry eyes and cataracts.
- Olive oil contains omega-3 fatty acids and antioxidants, which can help reduce inflammation and improve overall eye health.

In conclusion, this spinach and goat cheese omelet is a healthy and tasty option for a nutritious breakfast that can help improve eye health.

The ingredients are rich in nutrients and antioxidants that can help protect the eyes from free radical damage and prevent macular degeneration.

Try this simple and delicious recipe for a healthy and filling breakfast that can help improve your vision.

4. Vegetable Soup

Vegetable soup is a tasty and healthy dish that can help improve your vision thanks to the nutrients found in vegetables. This easy-to-make recipe is perfect for cold winter days or when you need a healthy, nourishing meal.

Here's the ingredient list and step-by-step instructions for making this delicious and nutritious vegetable soup.

Ingredients:

2 tablespoons olive oil

1 onion, chopped

2 cloves of garlic, chopped

2 carrots, peeled and cut into small pieces

2 stalks of celery, cut into small pieces

1 red bell pepper, cut into small pieces

1 zucchini, cut into small pieces

1 cup cabbage, cut into small pieces

4 cups of vegetable or chicken broth

1 can of diced tomatoes

1 tablespoon chopped fresh thyme

1 tablespoon chopped fresh parsley

Salt and ground black pepper to taste

Instructions:

In a large saucepan or casserole dish, heat olive oil over medium heat. Add chopped onion and garlic and sauté until translucent.

Add carrots, celery and red bell pepper and sauté for 5 minutes.

Add zucchini, cabbage, vegetable broth and diced tomatoes. Bring to a boil.

Reduce heat and simmer over low heat for about 15 minutes, or until vegetables are tender.

Add chopped fresh thyme and parsley and salt and pepper to taste.

Remove from heat and let cool for a few minutes.

Transfer the soup to a blender or use an immersion blender to blend the soup until smooth and creamy.

Ladle soup into bowls and serve hot.

This vegetable soup is not only delicious, but it is also rich in important nutrients for your eye health.

Carrots, celery and red bell pepper are rich in vitamin A, which is essential for retinal health and prevention of macular degeneration.

Cabbage is rich in vitamin C, which can help prevent cataracts and macular degeneration.

In addition, vegetable soup is an excellent source of fiber, potassium and iron, which can help improve the overall health of your eyes and body.

5. Steamed Broccoli

Steaming is a healthy cooking method that preserves the nutrients and antioxidants in food, and broccoli is a great vegetable for eye health because of its lutein and zeaxanthin content.

This simple steamed broccoli recipe is perfect for a healthy snack or tasty side dish.

Ingredients:

1 head broccoli

1 tablespoon of olive oil

Salt and pepper to taste

Instructions:

Thoroughly wash the broccoli head under running water to remove any dirt or impurities.

Cut the broccoli into small florets.

Boil about 2 inches of water in a large pot, then place a steaming basket in the pot.

Place the broccoli florets in the steamer basket and cover the pot with a lid.

Steam for about 5-7 minutes, until broccoli is tender but still crunchy. Check for doneness by poking the broccoli with a fork.

Remove the steamer basket from the pan with kitchen tongs and arrange the broccoli florets in a dish.

Add olive oil to the broccoli and season with salt and pepper to taste.

Serve hot and enjoy this delicious steamed vegetable.

Broccoli is rich in lutein and zeaxanthin, two antioxidants that can help prevent oxidative damage in the eyes and improve overall eye health.

In addition, broccoli is also an important source of vitamin C, which is another powerful antioxidant for the eyes.

Steaming preserves these nutrients and makes them more easily absorbed by the body.

This simple recipe is a great way to add healthy vegetables to your diet to improve your vision and overall health.

6. Stuffed peppers with quinoa and vegetables

Peppers stuffed with quinoa and vegetables is a great recipe to improve your vision.

Peppers are rich in vitamin C, which can help prevent cataracts and macular degeneration, while quinoa is rich in lutein and zeaxanthin, two antioxidants that help protect the eyes from free radical damage.

This recipe is also high in fiber and protein, making it a great choice for a healthy and satisfying meal.

Ingredients:

4 large red or yellow peppers

1 cup quinoa, rinsed and drained

2 cups vegetable broth

1 small onion, chopped

1 clove garlic, chopped

1 small zucchini, diced

1 small eggplant, diced

1 small tomato, diced

1/2 cup canned corn, drained and rinsed

1/2 cup canned chickpeas, drained and rinsed

1/4 cup grated cheese (optional)

Salt and freshly ground black pepper

Olive oil

Instructions:

Preheat oven to 375°F (190°C). Cut peppers in half lengthwise and remove seeds and membranes.

In a large saucepan, combine quinoa, vegetable broth, onion and garlic.

Bring to a boil over high heat, then reduce heat and simmer, covered, for 15 to 20 minutes, or until quinoa is cooked and all liquid has been absorbed.

Meanwhile, heat a small amount of olive oil in a skillet over medium heat.

Add the zucchini, eggplant and tomato and cook until the vegetables are tender, about 5-7 minutes.

Add the cooked vegetables, corn and chickpeas to the cooked quinoa mixture and mix well.

Season with salt and freshly ground black pepper.

Arrange the bell pepper halves in a lightly oiled baking dish. Fill each bell pepper with the quinoa and vegetable mixture, packing lightly.

Sprinkle grated cheese on top if desired.

Cover dish with foil and bake for about 30-40 minutes, or until peppers are tender.

Remove foil and continue baking for an additional 10 minutes, or until cheese is golden brown.

7. Grilled Salmon with Dill Sauce

Grilled salmon is a delicious and healthy recipe that can help improve your vision with the essential nutrients it contains, including omega-3 fatty acid, vitamin A and vitamin D.

Ingredients:

2 fresh salmon fillets

1 lemon

2 tablespoons olive oil

1/2 teaspoon salt

1/4 teaspoon black pepper

Dill sauce:

1/2 cup Greek yogurt

1/4 cup mayonnaise

1 tablespoon lemon juice

1 tablespoon chopped fresh dill

1/4 teaspoon salt

1/8 teaspoon black pepper

Instructions:

Preheat grill to medium-high heat.

Season salmon fillets with salt and black pepper.

In a bowl, combine olive oil and lemon juice. Brush salmon fillets with this mixture.

Place the salmon fillets on the grill and cook for about 6-8 minutes per side, or until the salmon is cooked through.

While the salmon is cooking, prepare the dill sauce by combining the Greek yogurt, mayonnaise, lemon juice, chopped fresh dill, salt and black pepper in a bowl.

Once the salmon is cooked, remove from the grill and serve with the dill sauce.

Nutrients and antioxidants:

Salmon is an excellent source of omega-3 fatty acids, which are essential for maintaining the health of the retina and macula of the eye.

It is also rich in vitamin A, which is important for corneal health, as well as vitamin D, which may help reduce the risk of age-related macular degeneration.

Dill, meanwhile, is rich in antioxidants, which can help protect the eyes from free radical damage. Greek yogurt is also a good source of protein and calcium, which can help maintain healthy bones and muscles in the eye.

8. Kale salad

Kale salad is a great option for improving your vision. Kale is rich in lutein, a powerful antioxidant that can help prevent free radical damage to the eyes. This simple yet delicious recipe is easy to prepare and can be served as a side dish or as a main course.

Ingredients:

1 bunch kale

1/2 cup walnuts

1/2 cup raisins

1/4 cup fresh lemon juice

1/4 cup olive oil

2 tablespoons honey

Salt and freshly ground black pepper

Instructions:

Wash the kale thoroughly and remove the center stems. Tear the leaves into small pieces and place in a large bowl.

Add the nuts and raisins to the bowl.

In a small bowl, mix the lemon juice, olive oil and honey until well combined.

Pour the dressing over the kale salad and toss well to coat all ingredients.

Add salt and freshly ground black pepper to taste.

Let the salad sit for 10 to 15 minutes to allow the flavors to meld and the kale to soften slightly.

Serve chilled.

Nutrients and antioxidants:

Kale is rich in lutein, an antioxidant that helps protect the eyes from free radical damage. It is also rich in vitamin C, which can help reduce the risk of cataracts.

Walnuts are rich in omega-3 fatty acids, which can help prevent age-related macular degeneration. Raisins are rich in antioxidants, including flavonoids, which may help protect the eyes from free radical damage.

Lemon is rich in vitamin C, an antioxidant that helps protect the eyes from free radical damage. Olive oil is rich in monounsaturated fatty acids, which can help prevent age-related eye disease.

9. Spaghetti with zucchini and tomato sauce

Here is the recipe for Spaghetti with Zucchini and Tomato Sauce, which is not only delicious, but also rich in nutrients and antioxidants that are beneficial for your eye health.

Ingredients:

4 medium zucchini

500 g of spaghetti

1 medium onion

4 cloves of garlic

1 can (400 g) crushed tomatoes

2 tablespoons of olive oil

Salt and freshly ground black pepper

Grated cheese for garnish (optional)

Instructions:

Wash the zucchini and slice into rounds.

Peel and chop onion and garlic.

Heat olive oil in a large skillet over medium heat. Add chopped onion and garlic and sauté until translucent.

Add zucchini to skillet and sauté for about 5-7 minutes until tender but still slightly crisp.

Add the crushed tomatoes to the pan and mix together. Add salt and freshly ground black pepper to taste. Simmer over low heat for 10 to 15 minutes until the tomato sauce thickens slightly.

Meanwhile, cook spaghetti according to package directions until al dente.

Drain spaghetti and add to pan with tomato sauce and zucchini. Toss until the pasta is well coated with the sauce.

Serve hot, topped with grated cheese if desired.

Nutritional information:

Zucchini are rich in vitamins C and A, which are beneficial to your eye health.

They also contain carotenoids, antioxidants that help prevent age-related macular degeneration and cataracts.

Tomatoes are rich in lycopene, an antioxidant that protects against oxidative damage to cells, including eye cells. Tomatoes also contain vitamin C, vitamin A and vitamin E.

Onions and garlic are rich in flavonoids and sulfur, which have anti-inflammatory and antioxidant properties beneficial to eye health.

So this recipe for spaghetti with zucchini and tomato sauce is not only delicious, but also beneficial to your eye health. Enjoy your meal!

10. Grilled Chicken with Vegetables

Here is the detailed recipe to prepare a delicious grilled chicken with vegetables that is not only tasty but also beneficial for your eye health:

Ingredients:

4 boneless, skinless chicken breasts

2 zucchini

1 red bell pepper

1 yellow bell pepper

1 red onion

1 lemon

2 cloves of garlic, chopped

2 tablespoons of olive oil

Salt and ground black pepper

Chopped fresh parsley for garnish

Instructions:

Preheat your grill to medium-high heat.

Wash the vegetables and cut them into evenly sized pieces.

In a large bowl, combine the minced garlic, olive oil, lemon juice, salt and pepper.

Add chicken breasts to the bowl and coat well with the mixture.

Add the vegetables to the bowl and coat well with the mixture as well.

Thread chicken and vegetables onto skewers.

Place the skewers on the preheated grill and cook for about 10 minutes on each side or until the chicken is cooked and the vegetables are lightly grilled.

Remove skewers from grill and place on a plate.

Garnish with chopped fresh parsley and serve hot.

Nutrients and antioxidants:

This recipe is high in protein from the chicken and fiber from the vegetables. The red and yellow peppers are rich in vitamin C, an antioxidant that can help prevent age-related macular degeneration.

Zucchini contains lutein and zeaxanthin, antioxidants that can help protect the eyes from free radical damage. Garlic also contains sulfur compounds that can help protect your eye health.

Olive oil is rich in monounsaturated fatty acids, which can help improve eye health.

11.pan-fried greens

Skillet greens is a simple, quick and delicious recipe that is packed with nutrients for eye health. This recipe includes greens like spinach, kale, broccoli, green beans and zucchini, which are rich in antioxidants, vitamins and minerals essential for maintaining good eye health.

Here are the ingredients and steps to prepare this skillet:

Ingredients:

1 handful of spinach

1 handful of kale

1 handful of broccoli

1 handful of green beans

1 zucchini

1 red onion

1 clove of garlic

1 tablespoon of olive oil

Salt and pepper to taste

Instructions:

Start by washing all the greens and cutting them into small pieces.

Peel the red onion and garlic and chop them finely.

Heat olive oil in a frying pan over medium heat.

Add the chopped red onion and garlic and sauté until soft and lightly browned.

Add the greens to the pan and mix well with the onions and garlic.

Season with salt and pepper to taste.

Cook the greens for about 10 minutes, stirring occasionally, until they are cooked but still slightly crisp.

This pan-fried greens are an excellent source of eye health nutrients such as lutein, zeaxanthin, vitamin A, vitamin C and zinc.

These nutrients help protect the eyes from free radical damage, reduce the risk of eye diseases such as age-related macular degeneration (AMD) and cataracts, and maintain good visual acuity.

Adding this mixed greens to your regular diet can help maintain eye health and improve your vision.

12. Asparagus and Spinach Frittata

Asparagus and spinach frittata is an easy and healthy recipe that is great for your eyes and overall health. Spinach and asparagus are rich in nutrients such as lutein and zeaxanthin, which are known to protect the eyes from free radical damage.

Ingredients:

6 eggs

1/4 cup milk

1/4 cup grated cheese (preferably Parmesan)

1 tablespoon of olive oil

1 onion, chopped

1 clove of garlic, chopped

1/2 cup asparagus, chopped

1 cup fresh spinach leaves

salt and freshly ground black pepper

Instructions:

Preheat oven to 200°C.

In a bowl, whisk together eggs, milk and grated cheese. Set aside.

In an ovenproof skillet, heat olive oil over medium heat. Add onion and garlic and cook until tender and fragrant.

Add chopped asparagus and spinach leaves to the pan. Cook until vegetables are tender and spinach leaves are wilted.

Divide the vegetables evenly among the pan and pour the egg mixture over the top.

Season with salt and freshly ground black pepper.

Bake the frittata in the preheated oven for about 15 to 20 minutes, or until the top is golden and the center is firm.

Serve warm or at room temperature.

This frittata is a great option for breakfast or brunch. The eggs provide high-quality protein, while the greens add fiber and a variety of eye-benefiting nutrients.

Grated cheese is a source of calcium, which is important for bone and eye health. You can also add fresh herbs, such as dill or parsley, to add extra flavor and further increase the nutritional value.

13. Tofu Vegetable Stir-Fry

Here's the detailed recipe for Vegetable Tofu Stir-Fry, which is a great option for improving your vision thanks to its rich nutrient and antioxidant content.

Ingredients:

1 block of firm tofu

1 zucchini

1 red bell pepper

1 red onion

2 cloves of garlic

2 tablespoons of olive oil

1 tablespoon of soy sauce

1 tablespoon of rice vinegar

1 tablespoon of honey

1 tablespoon cornstarch

Salt and ground black pepper to taste

Fresh cilantro, for garnish

Instructions:

Start by preparing all the ingredients. Drain the tofu and cut it into cubes. Also dice the zucchini and red bell pepper, chop the red onion and mince the garlic.

In a small bowl, mix the soy sauce, rice vinegar, honey and cornstarch. Set aside.

In a large skillet, heat olive oil over medium heat. Add the red onion and garlic and sauté for 1 to 2 minutes until soft.

Then add the tofu and sauté for 3 to 4 minutes until golden and crispy.

Add the zucchini and red bell pepper to the pan and sauté for 5-7 minutes until tender.

Pour the sauce mixture into the pan and stir well so that the vegetables and tofu are well coated.

Season with salt and ground black pepper to taste.

Garnish with fresh cilantro and serve hot.

Nutrients and antioxidants:

Tofu is an excellent source of vegetable protein and also contains essential nutrients such as iron and calcium. Vegetables are rich in antioxidants, vitamins and minerals. Red peppers contain vitamin C, which can help prevent age-related macular degeneration, while zucchini is a good source of lutein and zeaxanthin, two important antioxidants for eye health. By adding tofu and vegetables to your diet, you can improve your vision while enjoying a delicious meal.

14. Shredded Carrot Salad

Grated carrot salad is a healthy and delicious dish that can help improve your vision.

Carrots are rich in beta-carotene, an antioxidant that can help protect the eyes from free radical damage.

In addition to carrots, this salad contains ingredients such as raisins and walnuts, which are also rich in eye-beneficial nutrients.

Ingredients:

4 medium carrots

1/2 cup raisins

1/2 cup chopped walnuts

1/4 cup chopped cilantro

1/4 cup fresh lemon juice

2 tablespoons olive oil

Salt and freshly ground black pepper

Instructions:

Wash the carrots and peel them. Grate the carrots with a large hole grater.

In a large bowl, combine the grated carrots, raisins, chopped walnuts and cilantro.

In a small bowl, combine the fresh lemon juice and olive oil. Add a pinch of salt and freshly ground black pepper and whisk to combine.

Pour the dressing over the carrot salad and toss well to coat all ingredients.

Taste and adjust seasoning with salt and black pepper if necessary.

Refrigerate the salad for at least 30 minutes to allow the flavours to blend.

This salad is a great option for a healthy lunch or as a side dish for a light dinner.

It can be made ahead of time and stored in the refrigerator until you are ready to serve.

The nutrients and antioxidants in this salad can help protect your eyes and improve your overall vision.

15. Vegetable curry

Vegetable curry is a delicious and healthy dish that can help improve your vision.

It is packed with nutrient-rich ingredients such as vegetables and spices, which contain antioxidants that are beneficial to your eyes.

In this chapter, we will guide you through the ingredients and steps needed to make a delicious and healthy vegetable curry.

Ingredients:

2 tablespoons coconut oil or olive oil

1 red onion, chopped

3 cloves garlic, chopped

1 tablespoon fresh ginger, chopped

2 tablespoons red curry paste

1 teaspoon ground turmeric

1 teaspoon ground cumin

1/2 teaspoon ground cinnamon

1/2 teaspoon ground coriander

1 red bell pepper, diced

1 yellow bell pepper, diced

1 eggplant, diced

1 zucchini, diced

1 can of diced tomatoes

1 can coconut milk

1/2 cup vegetable broth

2 cups fresh spinach

Salt and pepper to taste

Chopped fresh cilantro, for garnish

Instructions:

In a large skillet, heat coconut or olive oil over medium-high heat. Add onion, garlic and ginger and sauté until soft and golden.

Add the red curry paste, turmeric, cumin, cinnamon and coriander and sauté for one minute.

Add the peppers, eggplant and zucchini and sauté for about 5 minutes until tender.

Add the diced tomatoes, coconut milk and vegetable stock and bring to a boil.

Reduce heat to medium-low and simmer for about 10 minutes, stirring occasionally.

Add fresh spinach and cook until slightly wilted.

Season with salt and pepper to taste.

Garnish with chopped fresh coriander and serve hot with brown rice or quinoa.

Vegetable curry is a tasty and nutritious dish that can be made with a variety of vegetables and spices to suit everyone's taste buds.

The vegetables used in the vegetable curry are rich in nutrients such as vitamins, minerals, dietary fiber and antioxidants that can help improve eye health

.

Common vegetables used in vegetable curry include potatoes, carrots, peas, green beans, onions and peppers.

Greens such as spinach, kale and broccoli can also be added for an extra dose of eye-friendly nutrients.

Spices like turmeric, coriander, cumin, ginger and cardamom not only add flavor to the vegetable curry, but are also rich in antioxidants such as curcumin, lycopene and quercetin.

These antioxidants can help prevent oxidative damage to eye cells and reduce the risk of eye diseases such as cataracts and macular degeneration.

Coconut milk is also often used in vegetable curries, adding a creamy texture and sweet flavor.

Coconut milk is a source of healthy fats that can help reduce inflammation and improve blood circulation, which can also help protect the eyes.

All in all, vegetable curry is a healthy and delicious dish that can help improve eye health due to its rich nutrient and antioxidant content.

By adding a variety of colorful vegetables and antioxidant-rich spices to your vegetable curry, you can create a tasty dish that can help protect your eyes and improve your vision.

16. Shrimp and vegetable skewers

Here is the detailed recipe for shrimp and vegetable skewers:

Ingredients:

24 large shrimp, peeled and deveined

2 red peppers, cut into 2 cm squares

1 zucchini, cut into 2 cm slices

1 red onion, cut into 2 cm squares

1 tablespoon olive oil

2 tablespoons soy sauce

1 tablespoon honey

1 tablespoon lemon juice

Salt and pepper

Instructions:

Prepare the ingredients by cutting the peppers, zucchini and onion into squares of about 2 cm.

In a bowl, mix the olive oil, soy sauce, honey and lemon juice. Add a pinch of salt and pepper and mix well.

Thread the shrimp, peppers, zucchini and onion onto skewers alternately.

Brush the skewers with the marinade and marinate for 15 to 20 minutes.

Preheat your grill or barbecue.

Grill the skewers for 3 to 4 minutes on each side or until the shrimp are cooked and the vegetables are tender.

Serve hot with a green salad or basmati rice.

Nutrients and antioxidants:

Shrimp are rich in vitamin D and omega-3, which are important nutrients for eye health.

Red peppers are rich in vitamin C, which can help prevent age-related macular degeneration (AMD) and cataracts.

Zucchini is an excellent source of lutein and zeaxanthin, two carotenoids that are known to help protect the retina from oxidative damage.

Red onions contain sulfur compounds that may help reduce the risk of developing cataracts. Soy sauce marinade also contains natural antioxidants, which can help reduce inflammation and protect the eyes from free radical damage.

17. roasted beet salad

Ingredients:

3 medium beets

1/2 cup walnuts

2 cups baby spinach

1/4 cup homemade balsamic vinaigrette

2 tablespoons olive oil

salt and freshly ground black pepper

Instructions:

Preheat the oven to 200°C.

Wash the beets and trim the ends.

Wrap each beet in aluminum foil and place on a baking sheet.

Bake for about 45 minutes to 1 hour, or until beets are tender.

Remove the beets from the oven and let them cool for a few minutes.

Meanwhile, toast the nuts in a skillet over medium heat for about 5 minutes, or until golden and fragrant. Remove from the pan and let cool.

Remove the foil from the beets and remove the skin with a knife. Cut them into small cubes and put them in a large bowl.

Add baby spinach, toasted walnuts and homemade balsamic vinaigrette. Mix well.

Season with olive oil, salt and freshly ground black pepper to taste.

Nutrients and antioxidants in the recipe:

Beets are rich in vitamin C, folate and potassium, all of which are important for eye health.

Spinach is rich in lutein and zeaxanthin, which can help prevent age-related macular degeneration.

Walnuts contain vitamin E, an antioxidant that can help prevent oxidative damage in the eyes.

Homemade balsamic vinaigrette is rich in antioxidants, such as polyphenols, which can help protect the eyes from free radical damage.

This roasted beet salad is a healthy and tasty dish that can help protect eye health with its nutrients and antioxidants.

It can be served as a side dish or as a main course. Enjoy!

18. Vegetarian Chili

Here is the recipe for Vegetarian Chili which includes ingredients, step-by-step instructions for preparation, as well as information about the nutrients and antioxidants in each dish and how they can help improve your vision.

Ingredients:

1 tablespoon olive oil

1 chopped onion

1 red bell pepper, chopped

2 cloves of garlic, chopped

1 can (15 oz) black beans, rinsed and drained

1 can (15 oz) kidney beans, rinsed and drained

1 can (15 oz.) diced tomatoes

1 can (15 ounces) corn, rinsed and drained

2 tablespoons chili powder

1 tablespoon ground cumin

1/2 teaspoon salt

Ground black pepper, to taste

2 cups water

2 tablespoons fresh lime juice

Chopped fresh cilantro for garnish

Instructions:

In a large saucepan, heat olive oil over medium heat. Add onion and red bell pepper and cook until soft, about 5 minutes. Add garlic and cook for 1 minute more.

Add black beans, red beans, diced tomatoes, corn, chili powder, cumin, salt and pepper. Mix well.

Add water and bring to a boil. Reduce heat to medium-low and simmer for 20 minutes.

Add fresh lime juice and stir. Simmer for another 5 minutes.

Garnish with fresh cilantro and serve.

19. Cauliflower Soup

Cauliflower soup is a creamy, delicious soup that is also rich in nutrients to improve eye health.

Cauliflower is an excellent source of vitamin C, vitamin K and carotenoids, which are important antioxidants for eye health.

Ingredients:

1 medium cauliflower, cut into small pieces

1 onion, chopped

3 cloves garlic, chopped

4 cups vegetable broth

1 cup of coconut milk

2 tablespoons olive oil

Salt and ground black pepper to taste

Instructions:

In a large saucepan, heat olive oil over medium heat. Add onion and garlic and sauté until soft.

Add cauliflower and vegetable broth and bring to a boil. Reduce heat, cover and simmer until cauliflower is tender, about 15 minutes.

Remove from heat and let cool slightly. Use an immersion blender to blend the soup until smooth and creamy.

Add coconut milk and return to medium heat. Heat the soup for an additional 5 minutes, stirring occasionally. Season with salt and pepper to taste.

Serve hot and garnish with fresh cilantro, if desired.

This soup is a great option for a healthy and nutritious dinner that not only tastes great, but will provide your eyes with essential nutrients to maintain their health.

20. Spinach and goat cheese pie

Ingredients:

1 shortcrust pastry

500g fresh spinach

1 onion

2 cloves of garlic

100g of fresh goat cheese

2 eggs

20cl of light cream

salt and pepper

Instructions:

Preheat the oven to 180°C.

Peel and chop the onion. Fry it in a hot pan with a little olive oil for about 5 minutes until golden.

Add the washed and drained spinach and the minced garlic. Cook over medium heat for about 5 minutes, until the spinach is softened.

In a bowl, beat the eggs into an omelette. Add the light cream, crumbled fresh goat cheese, salt and pepper. Mix well.

Place the shortcrust pastry in a pie pan. Prick the bottom with a fork.

Spread the spinach and onion on the pastry.

Pour the egg and goat cheese mixture over the spinach.

Bake for about 30 minutes, until golden brown.

Nutrients and antioxidants:

This spinach and goat cheese pie is an excellent source of vitamin A, vitamin C, and vitamin K, all of which are nutrients beneficial to eye health.

Spinach is also rich in lutein and zeaxanthin, two antioxidants that protect the eyes from UV damage and free radicals.

Goat cheese provides a source of protein and calcium for bone and muscle health.

The light liquid cream also contains healthy fats for the body.

21. Grilled white fish with tomato salsa

Here is the recipe for grilled white fish with tomato salsa:

Ingredients:

4 white fish fillets (cod, sole, etc.)

4 ripe tomatoes, diced

1 red onion, diced

2 cloves garlic, finely chopped

1/4 cup fresh coriander, finely chopped

2 tablespoons olive oil

1 tablespoon fresh lemon juice

Salt and pepper

Instructions:

In a bowl, combine tomatoes, red onion, garlic, cilantro, olive oil and lemon juice. Add salt and pepper to taste. Set aside.

Preheat grill to medium-high heat.

Season fish fillets with salt and pepper.

Place fish fillets on grill and cook for about 4 minutes on each side, until fish is cooked through and golden brown.

Remove the fish from the grill and serve hot, topped with the tomato salsa.

Nutrients and antioxidants:

This dish is rich in lean protein and omega-3 fatty acids, which are beneficial for eye health.

Tomatoes are an excellent source of lycopene, an antioxidant that can reduce the risk of age-related eye diseases such as macular degeneration.

Garlic is also rich in antioxidants that can help prevent free radical damage to the eyes.

Fresh cilantro contains vitamins A and K, which are important for eye health.

Finally, lemon juice is a source of vitamin C, which can help protect the eyes from UV damage and free radicals.

22. Fall Vegetable Stew

Here is the recipe for Fall Vegetable Stew, along with information on nutrients and antioxidants beneficial to eye health:

Ingredients:

2 carrots, sliced

2 turnips, diced

2 potatoes, cubed

1 onion, chopped

2 cloves of garlic, chopped

1 handful fresh green beans, chopped

2 cups of vegetable broth

1 tablespoon olive oil

1 teaspoon chopped fresh thyme

Salt and pepper to taste

Instructions:

In a large saucepan, heat the olive oil over medium heat. Add onion and garlic and cook until soft, about 5 minutes.

Add carrots, turnips and potatoes. Cook for 10 minutes until they begin to soften.

Add the vegetable stock, fresh thyme and green beans. Season with salt and pepper.

Bring to a boil, then reduce heat and simmer on low for about 20 minutes, until vegetables are tender.

Nutrients and antioxidants:

Carrots are rich in beta-carotene, an antioxidant that is converted to vitamin A in the body. Vitamin A is essential for healthy vision, especially for night vision.

Turnips are rich in vitamin C, which is a powerful antioxidant. Vitamin C can help protect the eyes from free radical damage.

Potatoes are rich in vitamin B6, which plays an important role in the production of melatonin. Melatonin is a hormone that helps regulate the sleep cycle and may have a beneficial effect on eye health.

Green beans are rich in lutein and zeaxanthin, two antioxidants that are naturally found in the macula of the eye. These antioxidants can help protect the eyes from blue light damage.

Fresh thyme is rich in vitamin C, a powerful antioxidant that can help protect the eyes from free radicals.

Enjoy your meal and take care of your eyes!

23. Grilled Chicken with Mango Salsa

Grilled Chicken with Mango Salsa

This recipe is a perfect marriage of fresh and juicy flavors, which is also beneficial for your eye health.

The grilled chicken is a source of lean protein, while the mango is rich in vitamin A and antioxidants.

The mango salsa adds a sweet and tangy touch that perfectly complements the grilled chicken.

Ingredients:

4 chicken fillets

2 ripe mangoes, diced

1/2 red onion, diced

1 red bell pepper, diced

1 small bunch of coriander, finely chopped

1 clove garlic, pressed

1 tablespoon fresh lime juice

1 tablespoon olive oil

Salt and freshly ground black pepper

Instructions:

Preheat your grill to medium-high heat.

Season the chicken fillets with a pinch of salt and black pepper.

In a bowl, combine diced mango, red onion, red bell pepper, cilantro, garlic, lime juice and olive oil. Season with a pinch of salt and black pepper.

Place the chicken fillets on the grill and cook for about 5-7 minutes on each side, until golden brown and cooked through.

Once the chicken is done, remove from the grill and let it rest for about 5 minutes before slicing.

Serve the grilled chicken with a generous portion of fresh mango salsa on top.

Nutrients and antioxidants:

Chicken is an excellent source of lean protein, which is necessary to maintain eye health.

Mango is a rich source of vitamin A, which is essential for good vision.

It also contains antioxidants such as carotenoids and polyphenols, which help protect the eyes from oxidative damage caused by free radicals.

Red onion and red bell pepper are also rich in antioxidants, especially vitamin C, which helps boost the immune system and maintain eye health.

24. Tomato and Mozzarella Salad

Here is the recipe for tomato and mozzarella salad:

Ingredients:

4 tomatoes

1 ball of mozzarella

A few fresh basil leaves

2 tablespoons of olive oil

1 tablespoon of balsamic vinegar

Salt and pepper

Instructions:

Wash the tomatoes and cut them into slices about 1 cm thick.

Cut the mozzarella ball into slices of about 1 cm thick.

Arrange the tomato and mozzarella slices alternately on a serving dish.

Wash and dry the basil leaves, then cut them into thin strips.

Sprinkle the basil leaves over the salad.

In a small bowl, mix the olive oil and balsamic vinegar.

Pour the dressing over the salad.

Season with salt and pepper to taste.

Nutrients and antioxidants in this recipe:

Tomatoes are rich in lycopene, an antioxidant that can help protect the eyes from free radical damage.

Mozzarella is a source of vitamin A, which is important for retinal health.

Basil contains vitamin A and lutein, which can help prevent age-related macular degeneration.

This salad is a healthy and delicious option for improving your vision. It is rich in nutrients and antioxidants that can help protect your eyes from eye disease.

25. Coral Lentil Soup

Coral lentil soup is a delicious recipe that is easy to prepare and very beneficial for your vision.

Coral lentils are rich in nutrients and antioxidants such as vitamin A, beta-carotene and lutein, which are essential for maintaining good eye health.

Ingredients:

1 cup of coral lentils

1 onion, chopped

2 cloves of garlic, chopped

1 potato, peeled and cut into small cubes

1 carrot, peeled and cut into small cubes

1 celery stalk, cut into small pieces

1 tablespoon grated ginger

1 teaspoon cumin powder

1 teaspoon turmeric powder

4 cups of vegetable stock

Salt and ground black pepper to taste

2 tablespoons olive oil

Chopped fresh cilantro for garnish

Instructions:

Rinse the coral lentils and set aside.

In a large saucepan, heat olive oil over medium heat and add onion, garlic, potato, carrot and celery. Sauté for 5 minutes or until vegetables are tender.

Add grated ginger, cumin powder and turmeric powder. Stir well and sauté for 2 minutes to release the flavours of the spices.

Add coral lentils and vegetable broth. Bring to a boil, then reduce heat and simmer for about 20 minutes or until lentils are tender.

Remove from heat and let cool slightly.

Pour the soup into a blender or use an immersion blender to puree it. If the soup is too thick, add a little hot water to reach the desired consistency.

Return the soup to the pot and reheat over low heat.

Add salt and ground black pepper to taste.

Serve hot garnished with chopped fresh coriander.

This coral lentil soup is a rich source of nutrients for your eyes, it contains vitamins A and C, as well as antioxidants such as beta-carotene and lutein that protect the eyes from free radical damage.

Vitamin A and beta-carotene are also important for maintaining good night vision and preventing age-related macular degeneration.

Turmeric is another beneficial ingredient that contains antioxidants and anti-inflammatory properties that help reduce inflammation in the eyes and improve blood flow, which can also help reduce the risk of eye disease.

In addition, this soup is an excellent source of vegetable protein and fiber, making it a healthy and nutritious dish for your body.

Coral lentils are rich in soluble fiber, which helps reduce blood cholesterol levels, improve digestion and maintain a healthy weight.

In summary, coral lentil soup is a healthy, delicious and easy to prepare recipe that can help improve your vision and overall health.

It is rich in essential nutrients for your eyes and contains powerful antioxidants that protect against free radical damage. Try this recipe now and enjoy all its benefits for your body and eyes.

26. Spaghetti with spinach and garlic

Here is the recipe to prepare spinach and garlic spaghetti, which is not only delicious but also rich in essential nutrients for your eyes :

Ingredients:

1 package of spaghetti

1 cup chopped fresh spinach

2 cloves garlic, finely chopped

1/4 cup olive oil

1/4 cup grated Parmesan cheese

salt and pepper

Instructions:

Bring a large pot of salted water to a boil and add the spaghetti. Cook according to package directions, or until al dente. Drain and set aside.

In a large skillet, heat olive oil over medium-high heat. Add chopped garlic cloves and cook until lightly browned and fragrant.

Add the chopped fresh spinach to the pan and cook until wilted and tender.

Add the cooked spaghetti to the pan and mix well with the garlic and spinach. Season with salt and pepper to taste.

Sprinkle grated parmesan cheese on top and mix well to melt.

Serve hot and enjoy your delicious spinach and garlic spaghetti recipe!

Spinach is rich in lutein and zeaxanthin, two antioxidants that are essential for eye health. These antioxidants can help prevent free radical damage in the cells of the eye and reduce the risk of age-related macular degeneration.

In addition, garlic contains selenium and vitamin C, which boost the immune system and protect the eyes from infection and disease.

Pasta is an excellent source of complex carbohydrates that provide energy to your body and help keep your blood sugar levels stable.

Parmesan cheese is an excellent source of calcium, which strengthens bones and teeth, and protein, which helps maintain muscle mass and repair damaged tissue.

In short, this Spinach and Garlic Spaghetti recipe is not only delicious, but it's also rich in essential nutrients for your eye health.

With powerful antioxidants, complex carbohydrates, calcium and protein, it's a perfect dish for maintaining healthy vision and overall good health.

So, try this recipe now and treat yourself while taking care of your eyes!

27. Meatballs with Vegetables

Recipe 27: Vegetable Meatballs

Vegetable meatballs are a delicious and healthy dish that can help improve your vision by providing a variety of essential nutrients to your eyes.

This recipe is easy to prepare and can be modified to suit your dietary preferences.

Ingredients:

500 g ground meat (beef or pork)

2 grated carrots

1 zucchini, grated

1 onion, finely chopped

2 cloves of garlic, finely chopped

2 tablespoons chopped parsley

2 tablespoons of flour

1 teaspoon of salt

1/2 teaspoon pepper

1 tablespoon of olive oil

Instructions:

In a large bowl, combine ground meat, grated carrots, grated zucchini, chopped onion, chopped garlic, and chopped parsley.

Add flour, salt and pepper. Mix well.

Form meatballs about 3 to 4 cm in diameter.

In a large skillet, heat olive oil over medium-high heat.

Add meatballs and cook for about 5 to 7 minutes, turning regularly, until golden and cooked through.

Remove meatballs from pan and place on a paper towel lined plate to remove excess fat.

Serve hot with a salad of greens or grilled vegetables.

Nutrients and antioxidants:

Carrots and zucchini are rich in vitamin A, which is important for eye health.

Vitamin A is an essential nutrient for the retina and cornea, and can help prevent cataracts and age-related macular degeneration.

Parsley is rich in lutein and zeaxanthin, two antioxidants that are important for eye health. These antioxidants can help protect the eyes from free radical damage, which can contribute to cataracts and macular degeneration.

In summary, this recipe for Vegetable Meatballs is a tasty and healthy dish that can help improve your vision by providing a variety of nutrients and antioxidants important for eye health. Try this easy-to-make recipe and enjoy it with your loved ones.

28. Chicken Curry with Vegetables

Recipe 28: Vegetable Chicken Curry

Vegetable chicken curry is a delicious and healthy dish that can help improve your vision by providing a variety of essential nutrients to your eyes. This recipe is easy to prepare and can be modified to suit your dietary preferences.

Ingredients:

500 g chicken breast, cut into pieces

1 zucchini, diced

1 red bell pepper, diced

1 onion, finely chopped

2 cloves of garlic, finely chopped

1 can of coconut milk (400 ml)

2 tablespoons of red curry paste

1 tablespoon of olive oil

1 tablespoon of honey

salt and pepper

Instructions:

In a large skillet, heat olive oil over medium-high heat.

Add chopped onion and garlic, and sauté for 2-3 minutes until lightly browned.

Add chicken pieces and cook for about 5 minutes until golden.

Add the vegetables (zucchini and bell pepper) and cook for 5 to 7 minutes until tender.

Add the red curry paste and stir to combine.

Add coconut milk and honey and stir to combine.

Reduce heat and simmer for about 15-20 minutes until sauce thickens and chicken is cooked through.

Add salt and pepper to taste.

Serve hot with basmati rice.

Nutrients and antioxidants:

Red peppers are rich in vitamin C, which is important for eye health. Vitamin C can help protect the eyes from free radical damage and can also help prevent cataracts.

Coconut milk is high in saturated fatty acids and calories, but it also contains important nutrients for eye health such as iron, magnesium and phosphorus.

These nutrients can help prevent cataracts and age-related macular degeneration.

Honey contains antioxidants such as vitamin C and vitamin E, as well as anti-inflammatory compounds.

These antioxidants can help protect the eyes from free radical damage.

In summary, this vegetable chicken curry recipe is a tasty and healthy dish that can help improve your vision by providing a variety of nutrients and antioxidants important for eye health.

It is important to note that this recipe also contains saturated fat from coconut milk, so it should be eaten in moderation if you are following a specific diet.

To maximize the eye health benefits, you can add nutrient rich vegetables such as carrots, spinach or broccoli to this recipe.

You can also modify the amount of red curry paste to adjust the amount of spice according to your preference.

In conclusion, this vegetable chicken curry recipe is a delicious and healthy way to take care of your eyes.

Try it at home to enjoy its health benefits while enjoying a tasty and satisfying dish.

29. Potato and celery root salad

This salad is not only tasty but also rich in nutrients for the eyes. Potatoes are rich in vitamin C and antioxidants such as lutein and zeaxanthin, which help protect the eyes from free radical damage. Celery root, meanwhile, is an excellent source of vitamin A, a nutrient crucial to eye health.

Ingredients:

500 g potatoes

1 medium celery root

1 red onion

2 tablespoons chopped parsley

1 tablespoon of mustard

2 tablespoons of cider vinegar

4 tablespoons of olive oil

Salt and pepper

Instructions:

Peel the potatoes and cut them into medium-sized cubes. Cook them in boiling salted water for about 15 minutes or until tender. Drain and set aside in a bowl.

Peel the celeriac and cut into small cubes. Chop the red onion. Add them to the potatoes in the bowl.

In a bowl, combine the mustard, cider vinegar, olive oil, salt and pepper. Whisk to make a smooth dressing.

Pour the vinaigrette over the vegetables in the salad bowl. Add the chopped parsley and mix well.

Cover the bowl with plastic wrap and refrigerate for at least 1 hour before serving.

This potato and celery root salad is a healthy and delicious option for caring for your eyes.

The nutrients in the potatoes and celery root, along with the mustard and cider vinegar in the dressing, can help improve your vision.

You can also customize this recipe by adding additional vegetables such as carrots or peppers to get more eye nutrients.

Enjoy!

30. Chicken and vegetable skewers

Chicken and vegetable kabobs are a great choice for an eye healthy diet. Chicken is an excellent source of protein, which is needed to build and repair eye tissue. Vegetables, on the other hand, are rich in antioxidants such as lutein and zeaxanthin, which help protect the eyes from free radical damage.

Ingredients:

500 g chicken breast

1 red bell pepper

1 yellow bell pepper

1 zucchini

1 red onion

2 tablespoons of olive oil

2 cloves of garlic

1 tablespoon of chopped rosemary

salt and pepper

Instructions:

Cut the chicken into medium-sized cubes and place them in a bowl.

Wash and chop the peppers and zucchini. Chop the red onion.

Add the vegetables to the chicken in the bowl.

Peel and finely chop the garlic cloves. Add them to the chicken and vegetable mixture.

Add the olive oil, rosemary, salt and pepper to the bowl and mix well.

Assemble the brochettes by alternating the chicken cubes and the vegetables.

Grill the brochettes on the barbecue or in a frying pan over medium-high heat for about 10 to 12 minutes, turning them regularly to cook evenly.

Chicken and vegetable skewers are a delicious way to get a variety of eye-catching nutrients.

Peppers, zucchini and red onion contain vitamin C and antioxidants such as lutein and zeaxanthin, which can help protect the eyes from free radical damage.

Chicken, meanwhile, provides protein to help repair and build eye tissue.

Try this recipe at your next barbecue and enjoy its eye health benefits. Enjoy your meal!

31. Green Vegetable Risotto

Green vegetable risotto is a tasty and healthy dish that can help improve your vision thanks to the nutrients and antioxidants found in green vegetables.

Here are the necessary ingredients and step-by-step instructions for making this delicious dish.

Ingredients:

2 cups arborio rice

1/2 cup dry white wine

6 cups vegetable stock

1 medium onion, finely chopped

2 cloves garlic, finely chopped

1 cup broccoli, cut into small pieces

1 cup asparagus, cut into small pieces

1 cup green peas

1 cup fresh spinach, chopped

1/2 cup grated Parmesan cheese

2 tablespoons olive oil

Salt and freshly ground black pepper

Instructions:

Heat the vegetable broth in a saucepan over medium heat.

In a large skillet, heat the olive oil over medium heat. Add the onion and garlic and cook for 5 minutes, stirring occasionally, until soft and translucent.

Add the rice to the pan and stir well to cover with oil. Cook for about 1 minute, stirring constantly, until the rice becomes translucent.

Pour the white wine into the pan and mix well with the rice. Cook until the wine is completely absorbed.

Add a ladleful of hot stock to the pan and stir well with the rice. Cook over medium-low heat until the broth is completely absorbed. Repeat this step until all the broth is used and the rice is creamy and al dente.

Add the broccoli, asparagus and green peas to the pan and mix well with the rice. Cook for 2-3 minutes, until the vegetables are tender.

Add the chopped spinach and grated Parmesan cheese and mix well. Season with salt and freshly ground black pepper to taste.

Serve hot.

Nutrients and antioxidants:

Green vegetable risotto is an excellent source of vitamin C, which can help protect the eyes from free radical damage. It is also rich in vitamin A, which can help maintain eye health and prevent eye diseases such as cataracts and age-related macular degeneration.

The greens used in this recipe are rich in lutein and zeaxanthin.

32. Fresh Fruit Salad

A fresh fruit salad is a healthy and delicious option for improving your vision. This recipe is packed with antioxidants, vitamins and minerals that can help protect your eyes from oxidative damage.

Ingredients:

2 apples

2 bananas

1 mango

1 kiwi

1/2 pineapple

1 cup of strawberries

1 cup of blueberries

1 cup of melon

juice of 1 lime

1/4 cup of honey

1 teaspoon of cinnamon

1/4 cup shredded coconut

Instructions:

Cube the apples, bananas, mango, kiwi and pineapple and place in a large bowl.

Add strawberries, blueberries and melon cut into small pieces.

Squeeze the juice of one lime over the fruit to prevent browning and mix gently.

In a small bowl, mix honey and cinnamon together.

Pour the honey mixture over the fruit and toss to coat.

Sprinkle shredded coconut on top and serve chilled.

Nutrients:

This fruit salad is packed with beneficial nutrients for your eyes. Blueberries are rich in anthocyanins, an antioxidant that can help protect your eye cells from oxidative damage.

Strawberries are rich in vitamin C, which can help reduce the risk of cataracts. Kiwis are rich in lutein and zeaxanthin, carotenoids that can help protect the retina.

Apples are rich in fiber and vitamin C, while bananas and mangoes are rich in vitamin A, which can help keep your eyes healthy.

Finally, shredded coconut is rich in lauric acid, a fatty acid that can help maintain healthy vision.

33. Grilled fish with orange sauce

Grilled fish with orange sauce

Fatty fish like salmon, tuna and mackerel are rich in omega-3 fatty acids, which are essential for good eye health.

This recipe for grilled fish with orange sauce is a delicious and healthy option for improving your vision.

Ingredients:

4 white fish fillets (such as tilapia or halibut)

2 oranges (juice and zest)

2 tablespoons of honey

1 tablespoon of Dijon mustard

2 tablespoons of olive oil

salt and pepper

Chopped fresh dill for garnish

Instructions:

Preheat grill to medium-high heat.

In a small bowl, combine orange juice, zest, honey, Dijon mustard and olive oil to create the orange sauce. Reserve half of the sauce for garnish.

Brush fish fillets with remaining half of sauce and season with salt and pepper.

Place fish fillets on grill and cook for about 4 to 5 minutes on each side, or until golden and cooked through.

Garnish with reserved orange sauce and chopped fresh dill.

Nutrients and antioxidants:

Oranges are rich in vitamin C, which is an important antioxidant for eye health.

The omega-3 fatty acids found in fish are also beneficial to eye health by reducing the risk of developing age-related macular degeneration and dry eyes.

The honey used in the sauce contains antioxidants and flavonoids that can help reduce inflammation in the eyes.

Dijon mustard also contains antioxidants and nutrients such as vitamin C and selenium, which may help reduce the risk of developing cataracts.

34. Roasted cauliflower

Cauliflower is a vegetable rich in vitamin C and antioxidants, making it a great choice for improving your vision.

This vegetable is also very versatile and can be prepared in many different ways.

This simple roasted cauliflower recipe is a great way to add variety to your diet while helping to maintain your eye health.

Ingredients:

1 head cauliflower

2 tablespoons olive oil

1 teaspoon of salt

½ teaspoon ground black pepper

1 teaspoon paprika

1 teaspoon cumin

2 cloves garlic, finely chopped

Juice of one lemon

Instructions:

Preheat your oven to 200°C.

Wash the cauliflower and cut it into small florets.

In a bowl, mix the olive oil, salt, ground black pepper, paprika and cumin.

Add the cauliflower florets to the bowl and mix well until each floret is well coated with oil and spices.

Spread the cauliflower florets on a parchment-lined baking sheet.

Place the baking sheet in the oven and bake for about 20-25 minutes, until the cauliflower florets are golden and tender.

In a small bowl, combine the minced garlic and lemon juice.

Remove cauliflower from oven and place in a large bowl.

Pour the garlic and lemon mixture over the cauliflower and toss gently until each floret is well coated.

Serve hot as a side dish or with rice and vegetables for a complete meal.

This roasted cauliflower recipe is not only delicious, but it's also rich in eye-benefiting nutrients such as vitamin C and antioxidants.

35. Sweet potato soup

Sweet potatoes are rich in vitamin A and beta-carotene, two important nutrients for your eye health.

This creamy, comforting soup is a great way to enjoy the benefits of sweet potatoes while warming up on a winter's night.

Ingredients:

2 large sweet potatoes, peeled and cubed

1 medium onion, chopped

2 cloves garlic, finely chopped

4 cups vegetable stock

1/2 cup fresh cream

1 tablespoon olive oil

1 tablespoon unsalted butter

Salt and freshly ground black pepper

Instructions:

In a large saucepan, heat the olive oil and butter over medium heat. Add the onion and garlic and sauté until soft and translucent.

Add sweet potato cubes and vegetable broth. Bring to a boil, then reduce heat and simmer until sweet potatoes are tender and easy to mash with a fork, about 20 to 25 minutes.

Remove the pot from the heat and use an immersion blender to puree the soup smooth. If you don't have an immersion blender, you can also transfer the soup to a blender and puree it in batches.

Add the sour cream to the soup and blend well. Season with salt and freshly ground black pepper to taste.

Serve hot with toasted bread crumbs and grated cheese if desired.

This sweet potato soup is a great way to enjoy the health benefits of sweet potatoes while enjoying a comforting and delicious soup.

Sweet potatoes are rich in vitamin A and beta-carotene, two important nutrients for your eye health.

The fresh cream adds a creamy texture and slightly sweet flavor that perfectly complements the sweet potatoes.

Enjoy this soup on a cool day or evening to warm up and improve your vision.

36. Cinnamon Apple Pie

Apple cinnamon pie is a classic dessert that not only tastes great, but also contains ingredients that can help improve your vision.

Apples, in particular, are rich in vitamin C and antioxidants, which can help protect your eyes from free radical damage.

Ingredients:

1 pie crust

6 medium apples, peeled and quartered

1/2 cup sugar

1/2 teaspoon cinnamon

1/4 teaspoon nutmeg

1/4 teaspoon salt

1 tablespoon lemon juice

Instructions:

Preheat the oven to 190°C.

Place the pastry in a pie pan and prick the bottom with a fork.

In a bowl, mix sugar, cinnamon, nutmeg and salt.

Add the apples and lemon juice and mix well to coat the apples.

Arrange the apple wedges on the pie crust, overlapping them slightly.

Sprinkle the sugar and spice mixture over the apples.

Place the pie in the oven and bake for 45 minutes or until the crust is golden and the apples are tender.

Remove the pie from the oven and let it cool on a rack.

Remove the pie from the oven and let it cool on a rack.

Nutritional Information:

This apple cinnamon pie is high in vitamin C and fiber, which can help maintain the health of your eyes. Apples also contain antioxidants, which can help protect your eyes from free radical damage.

37. Chicken Chili

Here is the recipe for Chicken Chili, which is not only delicious but also contains nutrients and antioxidants that are beneficial to improve your eye health.

Ingredients:

4 boneless, skinless chicken breasts, cut into small cubes

2 red peppers, cut into small cubes

1 onion, chopped

4 cloves of garlic, minced

1 can kidney beans, rinsed and drained

1 can diced tomatoes, undrained

1 cup chicken broth

2 tablespoons chili powder

1 tablespoon ground cumin

1 tablespoon dried oregano

Salt and freshly ground black pepper to taste

2 tablespoons olive oil

Instructions:

In a large casserole dish or deep skillet, heat the olive oil over medium-high heat. Add onion and sauté for 2-3 minutes, until translucent.

Add chicken and sauté for 5-7 minutes, until browned on all sides.

Add peppers and garlic and sauté for an additional 2-3 minutes, until peppers are slightly softened.

Add kidney beans, diced tomatoes, chicken broth, chili powder, ground cumin, dried oregano, salt and pepper. Mix all ingredients together.

Bring mixture to a boil, then reduce heat and simmer on low for about 30-40 minutes, until chicken is cooked and flavours are well blended.

Serve hot with brown rice or whole grain bread.

The nutrients and antioxidants in this recipe are numerous.

Red peppers, for example, contain carotenoids such as lutein and zeaxanthin, which are important antioxidants for protecting the eyes from free radical damage.

Tomatoes are rich in vitamin C, which is essential for eye health, while kidney beans are an excellent source of zinc, an important mineral for maintaining good vision.

Chicken, meanwhile, is a source of healthy protein that helps maintain healthy eye muscles and prevent age-related macular degeneration.

All in all, Chicken Chili is a healthy, delicious and easy to prepare recipe that offers a variety of nutrients and antioxidants that are beneficial to your eye health.

It's important to eat foods rich in these nutrients and antioxidants on a regular basis to maintain your eye health and prevent age-related eye diseases.

In addition, this recipe is also high in fiber, which is beneficial for digestive health and can help reduce the risk of chronic diseases such as diabetes.

Finally, this recipe is also suitable for people with food allergies or intolerances, as it is naturally gluten-free and dairy-free.

You can also customize this recipe by adding additional vegetables such as spinach or mushrooms to increase the nutrient and fiber content.

In summary, Chicken Chili is a healthy and delicious recipe that contains nutrients and antioxidants that are beneficial to eye health.

It's easy to prepare, customizable and suitable for people with food allergies.

Try this recipe for a healthy, satisfying meal that will help you maintain eye and body health.

38. Cucumber and Tomato Salad

Cucumber and tomato salad is a delicious recipe that is not only tasty but also beneficial for your eye health.

This recipe is rich in nutrients such as vitamin A, vitamin C and lycopene, which are known to help maintain eye health and prevent age-related eye diseases.

Ingredients:

2 cucumbers, peeled and cubed

4 tomatoes, diced

1 red onion, thinly sliced

1/4 cup balsamic vinaigrette

Salt and ground black pepper to taste

Instructions:

In a large bowl, combine the cubed cucumber, tomato and sliced red onion.

Add balsamic vinaigrette and mix well.

Add salt and ground black pepper to taste.

Refrigerate the salad for at least 30 minutes before serving.

This salad is simple to make and requires only a few fresh, healthy ingredients. Cucumbers and tomatoes are rich in vitamins A and C, which are important nutrients for eye health.

Vitamin A helps maintain corneal health, while vitamin C can help prevent age-related eye diseases such as cataracts.

In addition, tomatoes are rich in lycopene, an antioxidant that can help protect the eyes from free radical damage.

Balsamic vinaigrette also contains antioxidants that can help prevent chronic diseases and improve overall health.

In summary, cucumber and tomato salad is a healthy and delicious recipe that contains nutrients and antioxidants beneficial to eye health.

It's easy to prepare and is a great addition to any healthy meal. Try this recipe for a tasty salad that benefits the health of your eyes and body.

39. Vegetable Fajitas

Vegetable fajitas are a healthy and tasty recipe that contains a variety of vegetables rich in nutrients and antioxidants beneficial to eye health.

This recipe is easy to prepare and is suitable for those following a vegetarian or vegan diet.

Ingredients:

- 1 red bell pepper, cut into strips
- 1 green bell pepper, cut into strips
- 1 red onion, cut into strips
- 1 zucchini, cut into strips
- 1 eggplant, cut into strips
- 2 tablespoons olive oil
- 1 tablespoon ground cumin

1 tablespoon smoked paprika

1/4 teaspoon salt

1/4 teaspoon ground black pepper

4 corn tortillas

Instructions:

Preheat oven to 200°C.

In a large bowl, combine the red bell pepper, green bell pepper, red onion, zucchini and eggplant strips.

Add olive oil, ground cumin, smoked paprika, salt and ground black pepper. Mix well.

Spread the vegetables on a baking sheet and bake for 20-25 minutes, stirring once halfway through.

Meanwhile, heat corn tortillas according to package directions.

Top each tortilla with grilled vegetables and serve.

This recipe is rich in nutrients such as vitamin A, vitamin C, vitamin K and folate, which are beneficial for eye health.

Peppers, red onion, zucchini and eggplant are all rich in antioxidants such as lutein and zeaxanthin, which are known to help prevent age-related eye diseases such as macular degeneration.

In addition, corn tortillas are high in fiber and complex carbohydrates, making them ideal for a healthy, balanced diet.

The spices used in this recipe, such as cumin and smoked paprika, also add delicious flavor while providing health benefits.

In summary, Vegetable Fajitas is a delicious and healthy recipe that contains a variety of vegetables rich in nutrients and antioxidants beneficial to eye health.

It's easy to prepare and suitable for anyone looking to eat healthier.

Try this recipe for a healthy and tasty meal that can help improve your eye and body health.

40. Spinach Meatballs

This spinach meatball recipe is a delicious and healthy dish that can help improve your vision thanks to the antioxidants and nutrients in spinach.

This recipe is easy to prepare and suitable for meat and vegetable lovers.

Ingredients:

500g ground meat

200g fresh spinach

1 onion

2 cloves of garlic

1 tablespoon of chopped parsley

1 teaspoon of salt

1/2 teaspoon pepper

1 egg

2 tablespoons of olive oil

Instructions:

Preheat your oven to 180°C.

In a frying pan, sauté the chopped onion and garlic in olive oil until soft.

Add the fresh spinach and cook until wilted. Remove from heat and allow to cool.

In a large bowl, combine ground meat, parsley, egg, salt and pepper.

Add the cooked spinach to the ground meat and mix well.

Form meatballs about 3 cm in diameter.

Place meatballs on a baking sheet and bake for about 20 minutes, or until cooked through.

Serve hot and enjoy!

Nutrients and antioxidants:

Spinach is rich in antioxidants, such as lutein and zeaxanthin, which help protect the eyes from free radical damage.

It is also an important source of vitamins A and C, which play an important role in eye health by promoting the growth and repair of eye tissue.

Ground meat is an excellent source of protein, which helps strengthen the muscles of the eye.

Chapter 11: Fruits to eat often for your eyes

The benefits of fruit for eye health

In this chapter, we will focus on fruits that are particularly beneficial for eye health. Fruits are an excellent source of vitamins, minerals, antioxidants and other nutrients that can help improve your eye health.

They are also delicious and easy to incorporate into your daily diet.

The eye health benefits of fruit are numerous. Fruit is rich in antioxidants such as vitamin C, vitamin E and beta-carotene, which protect the eyes from free radical damage.

Free radicals are unstable molecules that damage the cells of the eye and can lead to eye diseases such as cataracts and age-related macular degeneration.

Fruits are also rich in flavonoids, which are plant compounds that have antioxidant and anti-inflammatory properties.

Flavonoids can help reduce inflammation in the eyes and improve blood flow, which can help prevent eye disease.

Here are some of the most beneficial fruits for eye health :

Berries: Berries are rich in antioxidants such as vitamin C and anthocyanins, which can help protect the eyes from free radical damage. Berries include strawberries, raspberries, blueberries, blackberries and cranberries.

Citrus fruits: Citrus fruits such as oranges, tangerines and grapefruits are rich in vitamin C, which is an important antioxidant for eye health. Vitamin C can help reduce the risk of cataracts and age-related macular degeneration.

Kiwis: Kiwis are rich in vitamin C, lutein and zeaxanthin, which are all important nutrients for eye health. Lutein and zeaxanthin can help protect the eyes from UV damage and reduce the risk of cataracts and age-related macular degeneration.

Mangoes: Mangoes are rich in vitamin A, which is important for retinal health. Vitamin A can help reduce the risk of night blindness and other vision problems.

Red and purple fruits: Red and purple fruits such as red grapes, cherries and plums are rich in anthocyanins, which are powerful antioxidants. Anthocyanins can help protect the eyes from free radical damage and reduce the risk of cataracts and age-related macular degeneration.

In addition to antioxidants, fruits are also rich in vitamins and minerals that are essential for eye health.

For example, oranges and kiwis are rich in vitamin C, which helps maintain the health of blood vessels in the eye.

Bananas, on the other hand, are rich in vitamin A, which is important for night vision.

Red fruits such as strawberries, blackberries and raspberries contain anthocyanins, a pigment that gives them their bright color and benefits eye health by improving night vision and helping to reduce eye strain.

In addition to their ability to improve eye health, fruit is also a healthy and tasty option to satisfy a sweet tooth.

Eating fruit instead of candy or cake can reduce your intake of added sugar, which can help maintain a healthy weight and prevent chronic diseases such as diabetes.

In conclusion, eating fruit regularly is an easy and delicious way to take care of your eye health.

The antioxidants, vitamins and minerals found in fruit are essential for preventing eye disease and maintaining healthy vision.

Fruit is also a healthy alternative to sugary snacks, which can help maintain a healthy weight and prevent chronic disease.

By simply adding a serving of fruit to your daily diet, you can help improve your eye and overall health.

Fruit to include regularly in your diet for good eye health
Fruit is an important source of nutrients for our bodies, including our eye health. In fact, the antioxidants and vitamins found in fruit can prevent eye disease and improve our vision.

In this chapter, we'll focus on fruits that should be a regular part of our diet for good eye health.

Citrus fruits are an excellent source of vitamin C, which can help prevent cataracts and age-related macular degeneration.

Oranges, lemons and grapefruits are also rich in bioflavonoids, which can strengthen blood vessels in the eyes and improve blood flow.

Berries are another important source of nutrients for eye health. Blueberries, in particular, are rich in anthocyanins, natural pigments that can improve night vision and retinal function.

Raspberries and strawberries are also rich in vitamin C and antioxidants, which can prevent eye disease.

Red fruits such as cherries, currants and black currants are also rich in antioxidants.

Cherries, in particular, are rich in anthocyanins, like blueberries, and can help improve blood flow to the eyes.

Exotic fruits such as mangoes, papayas and pineapples are rich in vitamin C and beta-carotene, a precursor to vitamin A.

Vitamin A is important for eye health because it can prevent night blindness and age-related macular degeneration.

Mangoes and cantaloupes are also rich in lutein and zeaxanthin, pigments that can protect the retina from light damage.

Finally, fruits rich in vitamin A, such as mangoes, apricots, melons and cantaloupes, are also important for eye health.

Vitamin A is necessary for the formation of visual pigments in the retina, which allow for clear, sharp vision.

It is recommended to eat a variety of fruits every day to benefit from the nutrients they contain.

Try to incorporate these fruits into your meals and snacks to improve your eye health. You can eat them as is, add them to smoothies or use them to make healthy and tasty desserts.

In summary, fruit is an excellent source of nutrients for eye health.

Citrus fruits, berries, berries, exotic fruits and fruits rich in vitamin A are all important for maintaining good eye health.

Eating a variety of fruits every day can help prevent eye disease and improve your vision.

Conclusion

Summary of Key Points

In conclusion, it is clear that taking care of your eyesight is essential to a good quality of life.

By incorporating eye yoga exercises and eye-healthy foods into your daily routine, you can improve your vision and prevent eye disease.

The book "40 Eye Yoga Exercises, 40 Recipes to Improve Your Vision" has given you a detailed introduction on how you can take care of your eyes in a natural and healthy way.

Eye yoga exercises are a great way to relax the eye muscles and reduce eye strain. They can be easily incorporated into your daily routine and are beneficial for all age groups.

The recipes in this book are delicious, easy to prepare and rich in nutrients and antioxidants important to eye health.

The ingredients used in the recipes have been carefully selected for their nutritional value and vision benefits.

Antioxidant-rich fruits and vegetables are especially important for eye health.

Berries, citrus fruits, green leafy vegetables and exotic fruits are just a few examples of antioxidant-rich foods that can help prevent eye disease.

In addition, it is important to maintain a balanced diet and stay hydrated for good eye health.

Excessive exposure to blue light from electronic screens can also cause eye strain, so it's important to take regular breaks and use blue light filters to protect your eyes.

Finally, it's crucial to see your eye doctor regularly for a comprehensive eye exam.

Regular exams can detect eye problems before they become serious and allow for early treatment.

All in all, this book is intended to help you understand the importance of taking care of your eyes and to provide you with natural and healthy ways to improve your vision.

We hope you have found these eye yoga exercises and eye recipes helpful and beneficial to your eye health.

Practical tips for integrating eye yoga and eye nutrition into your daily life
Integrating eye yoga and healthy eating can have a significant impact on your eye health.

Here are some practical tips for incorporating these practices into your daily life.

First, it's important to remember that your eyes need rest.

Avoid spending long hours staring at a computer or television screen.

Take regular breaks and practice eye relaxation exercises to help reduce eye strain.

In terms of diet,

Include antioxidant-rich fruits and vegetables in your diet on a regular basis.

However, keep in mind that some foods can be harmful to your eyes and should be eaten in moderation.

For example, foods high in saturated fat and sugar can increase the risk of eye diseases such as macular degeneration.

Similarly, excessive alcohol consumption can lead to optic nerve damage and impaired vision.

It's also important to make sure you get enough vitamins and minerals in your diet.

For example, vitamin A is essential for good vision and is found in foods such as carrots, spinach and sweet potatoes.
Similarly, vitamin C is found in citrus fruits, strawberries and kiwi fruit, and can help prevent cataracts.

Finally, don't forget to practice eye yoga exercises regularly. You can incorporate them into your daily routine by practicing them in the morning or at night before bed.

Over time, these practices can help strengthen eye muscles, improve blood flow to the eyes and prevent vision problems.

In short, incorporating eye yoga and a healthy diet into your daily life can have a positive impact on your eye health.

Be sure to take regular breaks to rest your eyes, eat foods rich in antioxidants and vitamins, and practice regular eye yoga exercises for healthy eyes.

Acknowledgements

Dear readers,

I would like to take a moment

to thank you for choosing my book

"40 Eye Yoga Exercises, 40 Recipes to Improve Your Vision."

This book has been an exciting and important project for me, and I sincerely hope it has been helpful to you on your journey to better eye health.

I would also like to thank all of the medical professionals who contributed to this book by sharing their knowledge and expertise.

Their advice and research were essential in creating a comprehensive and accurate guide to eye health.

I would also like to thank my family and friends for their constant support throughout this process. Their encouragement and enthusiasm have been a source of motivation for me.

Finally, I would like to thank everyone who worked hard to make this book possible, including the editorial team and designers.

Their dedication and expertise made it possible to create a professional quality book.

Thank you again for reading and I hope this book helps you maintain good eye health for years to come.

Sincerely,

Jean claude Mk.

Made in the USA
Monee, IL
20 October 2024